Nature Walk

Katie Peters

GRL Consultants,
Diane Craig and Monica Marx,
Certified Literacy Specialists

Lerner Publications ◆ Minneapolis

Lerner Publications Company
A division of Lerner Publishing Group, Inc.
241 First Avenue North
Minneapolis, MN 55401 USA

For reading levels and more information, look up this title at www.lernerbooks.com.

Main body text set in Memphis Pro 24/39
Typeface provided by Linotype.

Photo Acknowledgments
The images in this book are used with the permission of: © Shutterstock, pp. 3,
8–9, 10–11, 12–13, 14–15, 16 (top left), 16 (top right, bottom left), 16 (bottom right);
© iStockphoto, pp. 4–5, 6–7, 16 (top center), 16 (bottom center)

Front cover: © iStockphoto

Library of Congress Cataloging-in-Publication Data

Names: Peters, Katie, author.
Title: Nature walk / Katie Peters.
Description: Minneapolis : Lerner Publications, [2020] | Series: Science all around
    me (Pull ahead readers - Nonfiction) | Includes index. | Audience: Age 4–7. |
    Audience: K to Grade 3.
Identifiers: LCCN 2018058162 (print) | LCCN 2019000015 (ebook) |
    ISBN 9781541562288 (eb pdf) | ISBN 9781541558458 (lb : alk. paper) |
    ISBN 9781541573338 (pb : alk. paper)
Subjects: LCSH: Nature—Juvenile literature.
Classification: LCC QH48 (ebook) | LCC QH48 .P5228 2020 (print) | DDC 508—dc23

LC record available at https://lccn.loc.gov/2018058162

Manufactured in the United States of America
2-50511-46226-4/2/2021

Contents

Nature Walk 4

Did You See It? 16

Index 16

Nature Walk

We see a bird.

The bird flies away.

We see a stone.

The stone lies on the path.

We see a squirrel.

The squirrel eats a nut.

We see a stream.

The stream flows quickly.

We see a tree.

The tree grows leaves.

We see a bench.

We sit on the bench.

Did You See It?

bench

bird

nut

squirrel

stone

stream

Index

bench, 15

bird, 5

leaves, 13

nut, 9

squirrel, 9

stone, 7

stream, 11

tree, 13